NETWORK WITH PURPOSE

Transform Your Skills
In 4 Simple Steps

GORDON JENKINS

DEDICATION

To Wendy, my wonderful wife.

You had the vision, mindset, patience and belief in me that enabled me to overcome one of my biggest obstacles.

Make a real difference not an excuse.

With much love always, Gordon xxx

CONTENTS

DEDICATION iii

CONTENTS v

FOREWORD vii

PREFACE ix

MY STORY 1

WHY NETWORKWITH PURPOSE? 5

STEP 1: BE VISIBLE 19

STEP 2: BE MEMORABLE 31

STEP 3: BE INTRIGUING 39

STEP 4: BE COMPELLING 49

IN MEMORIAM 59

COPYRIGHT 61

FOREWORD

Gordon Jenkin's *Network with Purpose* perfectly encapsulates most people's anxieties around networking. It offers valuable insights on how to overcome these fears and network confidently and objectively. An indispensable read for anyone seeking to grow professionally and personally.

Marcel Kreis
CEO - E2Language
Former Chairman and Managing Director - Credit Suisse Private Banking Asia Pacific

PREFACE

When sharing my experiences about how I have grown teams and coached individuals to excel, either personally or with their business, one of the questions I often get asked is, "How do I become a better networker?"

I usually respond by asking, "What makes you think you are not a great networker already?"

The responses are usually something like, "I'm not an extrovert. I don't like going to networking meetings and standing in a crowd not knowing anyone. I go to a lot of events and meet many people, but they never seem to want to do business."

Unfortunately, I'm also seeing an increase in the following types of responses; "It's a critical part of my KPIs (Key Performance Indicators) and I'm not meeting the target," and "I'm all over social media, but I get no enquiries."

From these initial responses, I always delve further.

NETWORK WITH PURPOSE

"Share with me how you currently undertake networking? Give me an example of how you are genuinely focused on the other person instead of yourself? Explain in more detail what is your purpose for networking? How would it impact you if you were to transform and polish your strategy, so that you could actually achieve some short and medium-term outcomes for the challenges you mentioned?"

These people are already networking; they are just not approaching it with any purpose or structure. The crucial actions, accountability and outcomes are being overlooked because there is no framework in place.

The FEAR of networking is just that – False Expectations Appearing Real. Networking is so much more than just standing in a room, meeting people. Yes, this is a form of networking, however, you will be pleased to discover that it is also only one of many pathways to network effectively.

Network with Purpose is about adopting, implementing and measuring a framework that is timely in terms of relevance vs effort vs effectiveness. It is financially driven, enabling cost savings by networking more efficiently, and in turn improving financial growth, and

PREFACE

enabling individuals to network with freedom and in a way that suits their personal style. It will compel others to seek you out, not just today, but well into the future.

I believe that networking is a vital skill for people of all backgrounds. I originally developed my expertise out of necessity. However, over time, I found that networking has become an extension of me – my brand, my lifestyle. One of the compelling outcomes has been the opportunities to share my own experiences and insights with others who have a deep desire to make a difference or change, rather than offer excuses.

The overriding transformation is that Network with Purpose is always about THEM – not YOU.

You may not want to be a networking guru; however, I'm guessing you would at least like to feel more confident and assured when connecting with others. Networking can help build lasting relationships, give voices to those who were previously invisible, and can be the foundation of a successful leader or influencer.

> "Don't be a hostage to your past ways of networking. Trust your new journey."

Learn how to transform in four simple steps, as you master how to Network with Purpose.

MY STORY

In life, we've all gone through certain struggles. We've all had situations where we were ignored, or we didn't fit a particular system. We felt invisible. To give you an example, in my early school days I wanted to learn cooking, but the school system didn't allow boys to take cooking classes. I had to do woodwork instead. I would do what was asked of me in the woodwork class, but then I'd come home and bake a cake.

My 'invisibility' continued as I completed my education and launched into my career, I just didn't have a name for it at the time. I never felt like I fitted the mould, and instead was being carried down a path that was not of my making – a sheep following the shepherd.

For a long time, my life followed two parallel lanes; the first lane was governed by the way I progressed through life; successful but invisible. The other lane was my passion, the reason I wanted to exist. With both lanes running separately, there were many times I wondered whether life was worth living.

I believed that all I wanted was to be accepted, but later I realised I craved happiness and purpose. I lacked true direction until I stopped what I was doing, removed myself from the noise, and discovered my passion.

The catalyst was when my wife faced a life and death situation. She received all the care and support she needed, but I was left juggling work and carer responsibilities, and it felt as though no-one noticed the depth of my struggles. How do you raise an issue like this when others are fighting just to live? How do you say, 'What about me?' without sounding selfish?

In the end, my carer duties forced me to jump off the 'corporate gravy train' and develop my own business. I was invisible again, but this time I was more self-aware. I knew it was time to make some changes.

The journey I went on required me to reflect on what I was really passionate about, and in turn what I could offer to others by sharing my own story of being 'invisible'.

It is my belief that you need to step out of the shadows in order to fully participate in your life and the lives of those around you. It is never too late to live with purpose and passion.

MY STORY

You too can become visible, enabling you to move forward with your life in a way that you would never expect possible. I believe that with the right mindset, everyone is capable of incredible things.

Strengthened from my experience and expertise, I guide people to exceed what they think is their full potential.

Regardless of the shortcomings of the past, I am still grateful for every moment I have lived and the opportunity I have to share the most amazing experiences. The mindset of purpose is the single most important factor in why I am visible today and fully participating in life.

> "You can be visible too – do not stop believing just because others found an excuse."

Rather than going down the same path trodden by others, for the reward I thought I wanted, I am now creating my own path, my own journey, to get me to where I want to be.

Whilst I may still end up at the same destination as others, I will be true to myself, and take the path that is right for me.

WHY NETWORK WITH PURPOSE?

Looking back over the past 25 years, I've found that I excelled in environments that were very innovative and provided a platform for individuals to be inventive and to grow as leaders. And what I mean by 'leaders' is not necessarily people who want to manage others, but people who have ideas to help future-proof growth. One of my passions was enabling others to collaborate, motivate and influence others to implement these valuable ideas. I found that the most efficient way to do this is by learning how to network, whether internally or with third parties.

Want support from other team members? To be noticed by key influencers or potential clients? Be at the top of the list for a promotion? Want to get things done?

Learn how to network.

The problem is that many people don't like the idea of networking for a number of reasons. Perhaps they are fearful of saying the wrong thing, being rejected, having to engage in small-talk, being under the spotlight, having to mingle, or feel they are under pressure to connect and sell. Maybe they're there for the wrong reasons, wanting to sound knowledgeable, but at a loss as to what to say, not sure how to follow up, or worried what someone may think. The list can be endless.

Yet, we almost always agree on the value of networking, which is where our frustrations lie. Wouldn't it be great to have an expert show you a way to improve your networking skills?

After many years of honing my networking skills, I concluded that there were four key stages to networking in order to compel others into action. That's right – networking for a reason, not just networking for the sake of making new friends, although I have made many.

The Network with Purpose concept was born.

I came to Australia 25 years ago without knowing anyone, so I had to build a new network. My previous network in the United Kingdom was no longer relevant to my life in Australia. Subsequently, the network I created 25 years ago was vastly different to the one I have today.

WHY NETWORK WITH PURPOSE

So why is Network with Purpose such a key component of my philosophy? It is simply this; utilising tools to help you to exceed what you think is your full potential. What better way than harnessing the power of networking to enable you to construct the state of play that you desire?

I strongly believe that if people are forced into a group or structure, without the ability to change or leave it, they will tend to spend their time resisting inclusion.

They won't feel like they fit in.
They will feel invisible.
Their performance may suffer.
They may choose not to share their innovative ideas.
They are more likely to leave.

Network with Purpose gives organisations and individuals a framework that will foster the right behaviour and decisions, which will naturally increase the quality of communication, trust and commitment of individuals within the overriding guidelines of the group or organisation.

It is the glue that enables individuals to feel that they have the potential to bind their intrinsic motivations with the goals of the greater whole. It helps people to discover and align their passions with the group or organisation, so they feel like they belong and can make a difference. They feel like they are being seen and heard. They have a voice and the chance to influence change.

Network with Purpose is fundamental to the way individuals interact, internally and externally; team members, clients, prospects, suppliers, brand ambassadors, advocates and industry colleagues.

Turning up at a networking event, hoping to generate immediate business, is foolhardy. You may leave with a handful of business cards, but little more.

Yet, networking events are often what spring to mind when you think about networking. Given that this may also generate feelings of fear, insecurity and even panic, you will be relieved to discover that these events are also only one of the many pathways to network.

Firstly, we'll discuss a little about networking, of which I believe there are three types. The first one is operational – how you get the job done and how you work and interact with your colleagues. The second is personal; this is about your own development and how people see you as you grow. The third is strategic – how you position yourself.

WHY NETWORK WITH PURPOSE

Network with Purpose harnesses all three types of networking and draws from your DNA. It utilises the drivers that make someone want to jump out of bed each day. In doing so, the networking is more genuine and natural. It elicits better outcomes and aligns with your goals and purpose.

The question I get asked most often is, "How do I determine my purpose?" ... such a vital question on so many levels. Once you know your purpose, it will guide your life decisions, influence how you behave, provide a sense of direction, shape your goals, and give meaning to your life. If you do not have a purpose then you risk wandering aimlessly, chasing any shiny object that might fulfil you in the short term. You can probably picture someone just like this, who flits from one opportunity to the next, chasing someone else's dream or what they think they should be doing. Maybe that someone is you.

Network with Purpose is about understanding what makes you and your intended audience 'tick' in a way that positively transforms how others relate to you.

Transforming the way that people interact with you will strengthen your purpose and compel others to seek you out. It will generate more meaningful relationships, enhance communication, improve trust, help to deal with conflict, and ensure that the people you are connected with are on the same journey as you.

Mastering it is by no means easy. In fact, at times it will be very challenging, especially when we seek to differentiate ourselves. But it can be rewarding and fun.

Most importantly, your journey to transform your networking is in your own hands. Whether you have the desire to find that path is up to you. Who and what you surround yourself with is up to you. Who you choose to bring with you on the journey is up to you.

You don't fit the mould ... you create it.

> "There is no time like the present."
>
> \- Anonymous

We need to talk about the future now. Where you want to be, or where your organisation wants to be, in seven years' time.

WHY NETWORK WITH PURPOSE

For example, if you think that in seven years' time you want to be the partner of a firm, you need to start acting like that now.

If, in seven years' time you want to sell your business, you have to start developing your business to be how you want it to be by the end of the seven years.

If, in seven years' time you want to live near the beach, be self-sufficient and lead a carefree life, you have to start making life-changing decisions now.

If, in seven years you want a life that is without boundaries, free of time constraints and 'chains' holding you to a particular location, you need to start now to ensure this lifestyle is sustainable.

You need to start transforming. What and who you are now needs to evolve and grow. Networking is a key part of that shift.

If not now, then when?

> "Don't count the days, make the days count."
>
> - Muhammad Ali

Still need to be convinced that networking can have so many benefits? Maybe you are yet to appreciate the intricacies of networking with others. You're possibly thinking, "Well, I'm already very technically skilled in what I do. People will want to network with me." You may be a valued member of an industry organisation or committee. You may even already know a lot of people. That is a great start, because these are some of the cornerstones to networking growth. However, you need more than just technical skills, membership of the relevant groups, or a contact list with many names. You need 'soft skills' that enable you to go beyond your qualifications and job-specific skills.

Take for example the doctor who has all the required technical skills, but a terrible 'bedside manner'; or the teacher who has all the answers, but can't efficiently communicate with students. The salesperson who has the best offer available, but is just so focused on their sales bonus that the customer goes elsewhere. The health or wellness coach who knows all the right techniques, but has trouble attracting customers.

Think of the growth they could experience if only they could use a skill like networking to cultivate the interactions they desire.

WHY NETWORK WITH PURPOSE

Personally, I don't like the term 'soft skills', as it implies a weakness or that it is less important. In my opinion, 'soft skills' should be as highly sought after as technical skills. They should be seen as essential business and personal skills. Soft skills are in fact transferable, and will enable you to thrive in your work or industry environment, as well as in your personal life. They are attributes that will foster more effective interactions with your colleagues, clients, family and friends.

Network with Purpose is designed to cultivate and develop these essential skills that you need to have. When you connect technical skills with business and personal skills, there is no need to make outlandish statements about what you can offer. Your qualities will be naturally showcased. You will become a product of your product(s). This is the recipe to exceed even your own expectations.

Let's think about what this means for the future.

When you become a partner in a professional services firm in seven years' time, you already want to be delivering that million-dollar-a-year revenue, as this needs to be the platform from which to build. When you establish that exclusive health retreat in seven years' time you want to have already developed a large, loyal clientele, which will be the foundation of your business. You'll never reach the heights you desire if you don't have the skills to stand out from the crowd, communicate succinctly, inspire others, and compel them to act.

When you start adopting the Network with Purpose approach and linking your technical skills with your business and personal skills, your network will start watching you. In my experience, many will watch from the shadows, as unnerving as that may sound. But they will still be there, waiting until they are compelled to act and connect with you. They'll start emulating you. Duplication – that's how you'll know when the transformation process is really working, and you are mastering the skill of networking.

I truly believe that Network with Purpose can help you grow and thrive as you follow your chosen path.

Yet understandably, I know that many of you will have questions at this stage. How do you develop the skills? How do you transform? You may have fears or insecurities that are holding you back.

> "Fear kills more dreams than failure ever would have."
>
> - Suzy Kassem

WHY NETWORK WITH PURPOSE

These are some of the more common excuses I am given. To me, they are just obstacles to success. Do any of them resonate with you?

1) I don't know where to start.

2) I don't like the pressure of mingling in a crowd.

3) I'm not an extrovert.

4) I worry that others won't want to read what I've shared.

5) I don't know what my passions or purpose are.

6) I can't do it like you can.

"Do not stop believing you can do it just because others found an excuse."

You can transform with Network with Purpose's four-step transformation process.

- It will provide you with the freedom, time and resources to express yourself authentically to your world – you will become more Visible (Stage 1).

- You will learn to build your reputation and story – you will become more Memorable (Stage 2).

- It will give you the purpose and conviction that you need to build credibility – people will find you Intriguing (Stage 3).

- You will develop commitment and assurance – people will see you as Compelling (Stage 4) and will want to take action.

The path that you will start to develop will enable others to see you in a renewed light. You will start to hear things like, "Sam is reliable and driven," "Emma is capable and conscientious," "Mike is sincere and efficient."

Note that these descriptions are all business and personal attributes, not technical skills. There will be more focus on your attitude and intuition, and the way you communicate with others.

WHY NETWORK WITH PURPOSE

When you can showcase your passions, people will gravitate to you. When you can quantify your attributes, people will remember and trust you. When you can display conviction in your actions, people will find you intriguing. When you can compel people to feel like they need to act ... then you are mastering how to Network with Purpose.

So, how do we do this?

STEP 1: BE VISIBLE

Why is being visible important?

Let's visualise a lake, with many pink flamingos. Ask yourself, "Am I just another pink flamingo or am I that blue flamingo standing out from the flock?"

If you're just another pink flamingo, then you are what I call 'an expert in a vacuum'. You may be technically skilled; you may know your 'stuff', but nobody knows anything about you. They don't know you exist. You're just another body in the crowd. You are invisible.

However, if you're a blue flamingo then you will be noticed. Being visible is about standing out from the crowd. Contrary to what some people think, the best way to do this is not to make the most noise, to beat the loudest drum or show off all of your finest qualities. It is not about you at all.

Being visible is more than just turning up to a networking event or having a coffee meeting. You do not even have to have a conversation with someone to be visible to them. There are a range of methods you can use to be seen. They may notice you liking one of their social media posts or comments. They may learn about you from a mutual acquaintance. A video you post may capture their attention. The way others positively greet you will start to create their first impression of you.

If you do have the opportunity to communicate directly, then this can still be outside a formal networking environment. Face to face contact is the ideal opportunity to listen to others and discover what their own passions and values are; what their needs are; what purpose they have. As you learn about them you will gain visibility threefold:

1. They will feel a special connection with you, as you have taken the time to value them.

2. They will feel more confident sharing with you their time, money and freedom aspirations.

3. They will feel comfortable in further developing a relationship with you.

Notice the emphasis on 'feel'. People will always remember how you make them feel. It is timely to

STEP 1: BE VISIBLE

remember that people don't really care about what we know, but they care how you make them feel. That will then make you the centre of purpose; the reason they want to be on your plane, your path and our journey. This is a key cornerstone of Network with Purpose.

Let me put this in a way that may resonate further.

Consider the dating app, Tinder, where you swipe left and swipe right. Tinder is all about schmoosing. It's cold and it's impersonal. It's about you and taking care of yourself. It's fake. Both parties are only showing what they want each other to see, not their real lives and feelings. People are posing for other people. It's about collecting likes. Where is the long-term intrinsic value in that?

On the other hand, Network with Purpose is all about the other person and how they feel. You put people first and you put your focus on them. You work in a network that is aligned with their passions. You seek like-minded individuals with whom you can really connect emotionally. You nurture relationships that are sustainable.

Think about the process of being where you want to be in seven years' time.

NETWORK WITH PURPOSE

You need to begin by determining how best to be visible in your network, organisation or industry. You ideally want to connect and work with people who have the same values as you. Most importantly, you're looking for outcomes that will benefit both parties, so they will want to have an ongoing relationship with you. You want to take accountable actions that align to this philosophy. In turn you will become more visible.

A useful analogy to highlight the importance of being visible is to imagine an airport. Imagine your destination; you are about to board your plane.

Who in your current network do you want to take on the plane with you to your ultimate destination? Who are the new contacts that currently don't see you, and would benefit by coming onboard?

Who do you want on your plane?

STEP 1: BE VISIBLE

Remember to focus on your ideal destination. You may find that your current network is no longer as relevant to your future. You may need to leave them at the departure gate. You can still remain friends, however, a long-distance relationship can be difficult when you are both heading in different directions.

I have found that there are five key challenges to being visible.

The first challenge is the need to be clear about what sets you apart from the market. What will make you more visible than others? You need to stay away from terms such as; we are your local professional in the suburbs, we are authentic, genuine, unique, dynamic, client-focused...

These are generic terms that everyone uses to try to stand out. It would be like describing a flamingo as pink, tall and covered in feathers. At the end of the day you're just one of the flock.

You need to be clear about what differentiates you. What can you quantify that will enable you to be credible? What have you actually done to help others in the past? How have you made them feel? What solutions did you specifically provide that helped them to realise their goals?

The second challenge is about transparency – how visible you will be? The stakeholders (people who are internal and external), want a high level of transparency.

They want to be clear on who you are, who they are, and who they are dealing with. They want to see who and what they are getting involved with. The transparency is not just in what you say, but also in how you act.

The third challenge is about staying relevant – how visible you are in the current environment? We live in an ever-changing and fast-moving world. The demographics are challenging organisations to stay relevant. The community that we're working in changes constantly.

STEP 1: BE VISIBLE

Technology is one of the biggest adaptive disruptors to humankind today.

More importantly, as we've said previously, the network of yesterday might not be the network of your future. As I previously mentioned I am a classical example of that. The network I had during the late 1990's during my investment banking career is almost irrelevant to my network today. I have had to re-establish my network. I am on a different plane, and I am moving in a different direction. The passengers who are onboard with me now are those who are relevant to my current journey.

The fourth challenge is the level of expectations – what are people expecting from us? How is your visibility going to be received? Employees, clients and the communities we live and work in are changing. They're anticipating and often demanding that everything we do will be focused upon them. It is important to have a client-centric model incorporating these expectations around what you're going to deliver. It's important to understand that today there could be five or six generations working in your organisation, from Generation Z and back.

We need to be able to work together. We need to understand that everyone has different passions and needs. The way that we want to be rewarded for our achievements varies. It is important to understand these factors, as there is a strong connection between intrinsic motivation of individuals and the direction of the business.

Perhaps the biggest challenge we face is the fifth, future-proofing our growth. Will you be visible for a fleeting moment or will your visibility endure?

Change can be very unsettling, but it needs to be our priority. If you're not changing, you're not growing. We need to start living now the way we want to live in seven years' time. We have to think about the actions we take today and ask, do they represent the way we want to be in seven years' time?

> "The destination won't get you
> to where you want to be. The journey will."

There are over twenty-one pathways to being visible. Attending a networking event is only the tip of the iceberg. No matter which path you take, what you do when you get there is key. It's a bit like collecting business cards. It's not the number of business cards you collect that is important, but what you do with them.

STEP 1: BE VISIBLE

The twenty-one pathways involve more than just face-to-face meetings, and more than just going into a room full of strangers and saying "Hello, I'm Gordon Jenkins. Here's my business card, can I have yours?" The twenty-one pathways connect your passions and purposes with your target market.

Let me talk about three simple pathways to being visible; school committees, podcasts and industry publications. Do you have children? School committees are a logical pathway for you to network. Do you like speaking into a microphone? Podcasts may be an ideal way to reach out to others. Do you like writing articles? Industry publications could be a useful medium for building your network.

In each of these pathways, you're going to be connecting either directly to your target market, or finding ambassadors or influencers for your chosen market. Now, you may be thinking that being visible in these pathways is simple, and perhaps you do this already. A few of you may have had some success, but a lot of you will still be learning the skills.

The question I pose is, what are the actions you're taking to be visible? Have you thought about the rationale behind what you are doing? What's the purpose? How do you know if these are the right actions to achieve your goals? Are you consistently visible with accountability around your approach? What outcomes are you having? It's more than just activity that's vital – it's the outcomes of the activity that matter.

Turning up to a committee meeting, but not connecting to others won't make you visible. Speaking to someone who has different goals may be interesting, but do you really want to be visible as a guest on their podcast series if their target audience is not the same as yours?

Writing articles on topics that you're not really passionate about may make you visible, but at what cost if the result is a non-authentic article.

STEP 1: BE VISIBLE

Learning how to be visible is challenging. However, the first step to Network with Purpose is to be genuinely interested and focused on the needs and feelings of others.

STEP 2: BE MEMORABLE

Once you have acquired the skill of becoming visible, you then need to be memorable. Why? You can learn how to be more visible, however, this will only be valuable if people remember you. There is little to be gained by spending time communicating with someone if the person then wonders who you are when you get in touch again later. Not only is it awkward for both parties, it is detrimental to all the ground work you have done. There is no point in having a presence online or within the industry, if it's only fleeting.

You may be thinking that if you are visible enough then they should remember you. Yes, they may recall you because you posted an outrageous story, have a striking profile photo, were full of positive energy at a party, or had a killer opening sentence.

But are these good reasons for them to remember you? The next time they need a service provider, will they think of the person who posted the outrageous story, or will they think of your competition because their product or service was more memorable?

You want to be visible, but for the right reasons.

What impression do people have of you? Think about simple things, like a DIY project at home that you might have commenced, but not finished. Think about a project at work that you might have started, but others had to complete it on your behalf. What impression does that give? You may be memorable, but for the wrong reasons.

People will only remember you if they have a reason to do so. In today's society, people are interested in what's in it for them. You need to demonstrate something of significance that is aligned to their needs, so they associate you with value, and you are the first to come to mind.

A friend of mine surmised that people only remember you if you owe them money, they find you attractive, or you have something they want. I believe there is some truth to this. It is referred to as 'memory by association'.

Ideally, you want people to have a long-term memory of you, so they can subconsciously recall you many months

STEP 2: BE MEMORABLE

or years down the track. I have had clients come to me after several years when they're finally ready to employ my services. After all that time, they remembered how I made them feel, and what was in it for them. They may have remembered a particular article that really resonated with them, or a positive comment I made after hearing one of their speeches. You never know when your network will need you, or when the time will be right for your network to contact you.

Remaining memorable for such a long time can be challenging, especially if you are still learning to network. A more effective approach is to work towards being memorable for different reasons.

This requires being consistent in the benefits you offer, and also demonstrating that you can deliver value in different ways. Don't just rely on a single approach. A multiple-pronged approach will strengthen the association in their mind.

How do people remain consistently memorable in the eyes of their network, and for the right reasons?

It could be a mix of both digital marketing and traditional marketing. You could be posting valuable content on

LinkedIn, but also be attending conferences, lunches and functions in person and offering words of wisdom or support. It could be utilising your ambassadors, and ensuring that they talk about you positively in the right networks. It may be connecting and referring people, or simply taking the time to compliment them. A sincere compliment is a powerful way to enrich a relationship and make someone remember you favourably.

Best of all, it's free.

As discussed, one of the key challenges to remain memorable is to ensure that you continually demonstrate what's in it for them. You need to communicate in a way that quantifies the value that you are going to give them.

If you're offering to connect them with another person, explain how they will benefit, instead of just saying, "You should meet Joe". If you're providing some tips, frame them in terms of a real-life example that you were involved with. Best of all is to have third party validations and, at the very least, detailed examples of why you are the expert they need to remember.

This is not your generic elevator pitch.

STEP 2: BE MEMORABLE

Quite often I see people coming out with their standard elevator pitch, but it's completely wrong for their current purpose or the environment they're in.

Likewise, showcasing your latest 'win' may seem like the right thing to do to impress people. However, if you have not taken the time to understand the audience you're networking with, you may be completely off the mark. Consider the individual who wants to start their own firm, and is looking for support, but they don't want their peers to know. Your 'pitch' to them as an employee may just fall short, in which case you will become just another 'expert' they won't remember for the future.

I want to share with you three examples of ways that you can be memorable on a consistent basis by using the power of association.

The first is to ask a different client each month to do a 30-second testimonial on the phone to say what outcomes they've generated for their business as a result of being a client of yours.

They're not necessarily going to say specifically what they've done or what you've done, but they're going to be talking about their outcomes; outcomes that others can relate to, and in turn people will remember you as being involved by association.

The second relates to work I undertook for an accounting firm. One of the testimonials we got back from one of their clients said that, before they engaged this accounting firm, their business was virtually insolvent, but their business was now profitable. There were real feelings and relief behind this statement. Again, they didn't actually say what the accountants had done, but when you hear a story with genuine and positive emotion, something sticks in the back of your mind. That is the type of accountant I want to work with. Feelings are a powerful form of association.

STEP 2: BE MEMORABLE

Another way that I try to be memorable is to send out cards to some of my prospects and clients. Recently I've been trying to pitch to a firm in Australia. I initially strove to become very visible to them, and then to become memorable.

I started following them and interacting with them on social media. We agreed to catch up, but we weren't able to for a few months.

They recently won an award and, rather than doing what everyone was doing and congratulate them on LinkedIn, I took the effort to send them a card which said, "Congratulations on winning the award, congratulations to the team and I look forward to seeing you in a few months' time." That was it, nothing else. The client simply took a picture of the card on their desk, sent me an SMS with the words "Impressive, look forward to talking to you." The client now associates me with a positive moment in their own journey.

That is how you become visible then memorable in a very competitive and over-exposed marketplace.

STEP 3: BE INTRIGUING

Intrigue occurs when people start to seek you out because they want to learn more from you. They remember you as the expert, the font of knowledge, the centre of the network, or, as I sometimes like to say, you're seen as 'the prize'. It signals that you're doing something right, that you're an influencer. You've got credibility. You're the person to go to, and who people want to be near.

Let's be honest; there's nothing better for one's ego than when people pursue you because they want to work or connect with you. It is certainly easier and cheaper than chasing them. It also gives you the potential to command a higher value for the services that you provide.

So how do you intrigue them?

Firstly, it's important to understand the challenges associated with being an intriguing person. It is very easy to revert back to the 'me' mentality when their focus is on you. Reflect on what we talked about regarding

Tinder; the schmoosing, it's about me, it's about likes. They're coming to you because they saw something that fascinated them. Perhaps it is because of something memorable that you've done. Maybe it's the way you engaged with someone, or the way you influenced a group of people. More often, it's due to the way you made them feel. They want more of that.

What is the right formula for being intriguing? Is there actually a formula?

There is no specific or easy solution, but there are a number of actions or traits that can highlight you in an attractive way that draws people in. What best intrigues them will depend on many factors. So, how do you know which to use? You employ the knowledge you have gained by becoming visible and memorable. You continue to focus on the other person. You continue to Network with Purpose.

For example, you could showcase your expertise by giving them a snapshot of how you would tackle a specific problem they've raised with you. Or you could share some research on a topic you know is of interest to them; it may be an image or article that will captivate them. Or you could mention an award that a client won, who is in their

STEP 3: BE INTRIGUING

same industry. In most cases, less is more. You want to share enough so that it captures their interest, but still leaves them wanting to hear or learn more; a reason for them to employ your services.

Creating intrigue involves a mixture of curiosity, opportunity and influence. Similar to baking a cake, you can have all the right ingredients, but unless you know how much and when to add each ingredient, your cake could end up being as flat as a pancake, or an impressive sponge cake. For Tinder fans, a swipe left (flat pancake) or right (sponge cake!).

Like a cake, but certainly not Tinder, building intrigue usually takes time and careful nurturing. It's not just the baking that is important. It's making the whole cake attractive so that, as the person experiences the layers of your cake, they want more of it, not just one slice. They want the whole cake, and the next and the next. You may as well open a bakery, as they would be your best customer!

The key to intrigue is that it is developed organically and remains interesting, authentic and pleasurable.

While on the topic of baked goods, let us utilise a technique of modern dating by taking 'breadcrumbing' and applying it to a non-dating context.

According to the Urban Dictionary, 'breadcrumbing' is 'the act of sending out flirtatious but non-committal text messages (i.e. 'breadcrumbs') in order to lure a partner without expending much effort'.

If you overload your client, prospect or target with too much information, it becomes uncomfortable. This is not intriguing – it is overwhelming.

When you drop 'breadcrumbs', things appear more casual and natural. It subtly heats up the conversation and interaction without looking like you're trying too hard. You want to Network with Purpose, not intensity and pace.

STEP 3: BE INTRIGUING

When should you start building intrigue by dropping breadcrumbs?

Throughout the relationship, you want to increase their fascination with you, however, you focus on developing it when you are visible and memorable to them. They will only follow your breadcrumb trail if they see value in the crumbs.

What does this look like in reality?

It is not, "Hi. I've been the manager of this health retreat for around 12 months. I moved here from London and I'm totally responsible for the operations and growth of the entire business. I know everything about the industry. Our clients spend anything from 1 hour to 3 days with us. You should try it out; it can resolve all your problems. By the way, what do you do?"

The prospect is likely to think, "Too much information, too soon; all about you, nothing about me. Oh, and by the way, you have already assumed I've got a few 'problems."

So, how should the breadcrumbing work in practice? Remember, it's all about intriguing snippets of conversation, building on being visible and memorable.

You start by focusing on their passion. What gets them up in the morning? They will be curious why you have asked this question, instead of asking what they do; breadcrumb number one. They will then usually be polite and ask the same of you, or at least what you do.

This is your opportunity to fascinate them with your reply and drop the second breadcrumb. Then it's back to focusing on them. Find out if the person has been to a retreat themselves. Ask open-ended questions to understand more about their needs and desires.

Hone in on their feelings. Be genuinely interested in their reasons, as this will give you useful insights, and you will start to comprehend what is important to them. Along the way you can offer them further observations, but only if relevant and of value. Make them aware that you find their answers important and valuable.

This is only the start of developing the relationship, and it's the start of the breadcrumb trail. With each subsequent communication, whether in person, online or indirectly, you will continue to drop breadcrumbs. The next article you write, or post you share, may be with them in mind. It could also be the next story you share in a mutual group, or the next survey, question or poll. It also

STEP 3: BE INTRIGUING

will be more efficient if you operate within a niche area, as the same breadcrumb will be attractive to a range of prospects.

Humans are interesting and inquisitive beings, and we like to ask questions. If a prospect is intrigued but too intimidated or fearful to ask you questions, then you have both hit a roadblock. It is absolutely critical that we make our contacts, colleagues, clients and community comfortable to ask questions – to enquire because they are curious (in a positive way) of what we are saying and the actions we are taking. In simple terms, we want them to pick up the breadcrumbs we are dropping, and ask for the cake.

You need to focus on why they're seeking you. You need to understand what their perception is, or what problem they think you can solve for them.

If you have successfully become visible and memorable to them for the right reasons, this should be congruent. If not, you need to redevelop the relationship before continuing.

Always remember, it's something that you've said or done during the visible or memorable stage that has made them want more. You need to find out what this is and duplicate it. When you create intrigue that causes people to seek you out, they're subconsciously saying they want to be on your plane. They want to join you on your journey. Now you just need to decide whether you want them on your plane. It's okay to have built a visible and memorable presence, and then realise that they're not the right fit after all.

Earlier, we talked about being the person or having the business you want in seven years, and that the network you have now might not be the network you need to grow your business. Not everyone that seeks you out will be a person you want to have in your network. It can take an investment in time and energy to determine this, unless you have an uncanny ability to understand people within a few minutes.

It also requires an effort to determine what generally intrigues others about you. This is valuable information. When people flock to you, take the time to find out what attracted them. If you find a common thread, then you have a platform to build from. If you're attracting them for the wrong reasons, then it's time to make some changes.

STEP 3: BE INTRIGUING

I've found that my aptitude for understanding people often intrigues others. A comment I often hear is, "You know people so well. How do you do that?"

Let me take you back to the example of the pink flamingos and combine it with the classical example of networking in a room full of people.

As mentioned, an event often jumps to mind when someone mentions networking, but this is something that only a few of us enjoy.

The room is full of pink flamingos and I'm that blue flamingo. Why? My opening question is usually "Hi, <name>, it's awesome to meet you. Did anyone or anything make you smile today?" My question engages instantly and creates a smile or laugh. Why? I care who they are, not what they are.

People will see me talking to others, laughing and joking, and inquiring about individuals. They will notice me asking lots of questions and doing a lot of listening. They will also see me introducing people, which I do to create intrigue.

People will often come up to me and ask, "Wow, Gordon, how did you get to know so many people in this room?"

I may actually not know a lot of people in the room, but what I do know is that attendees are there because they are interested in the other people in the room. So, one of the ways I use to become intriguing is to connect people, even if we've only just met. Why? It builds upon the reasons why people want to be in my circle of influence; why they want to board my plane. Their perception is that I can help them achieve their goal, their purpose for being in that room.

They are starting to be compelled to act.

STEP 4:
BE COMPELLING

After having absorbed the first few chapters, you should now be more appreciative of the networking journey that needs to occur before an individual will be compelled to act. The 'act' is whatever purpose you have set out to achieve. Is your purpose to compel them to purchase, sign up to a membership, want more information, or become a 'raving fan'? Without a clear purpose, how will you know if you've achieved it?

The time it takes to improve your networking skills will vary depending on your mindset and desire, however, all of the stages we have mentioned so far are equally important.

> "sUccess all depends on the second letter."
>
> - Anonymous

For example, a prospect may have reached the stage of being intrigued, yet they're still not compelled to act. No matter what you try, you just can't get them to the final stage. What will make them cross the line? How do you network with them so that you are compelling?

If this occurs, the key is to focus on what is holding them back, or what is acting as a roadblock. It's often a result of you not having given them the assurances they need. It's all very well being a visible, memorable and intriguing persona or business, but if they don't have the reassurances that you will do what you promise, or deliver what you claim, you will never get them to take the plunge.

As well as being intriguing, you need to be seen as trustworthy, genuine and a relatively 'safe' bet, especially if they have not used your service before. You need to have integrity and proof that you can deliver what you promise. Some individuals may take longer to feel confident enough to take the final step.

Rushing someone to act in that circumstance will backfire, and you will undo all the networking success you have had so far.

It's also timely at this stage to review the process; your thinking, and the actions that you have taken so far. You need to be continuously visible, memorable and intriguing. It may take a day, a month or a year before

STEP 4: BE COMPELLING

circumstances arise where an individual is compelled to seek you out.

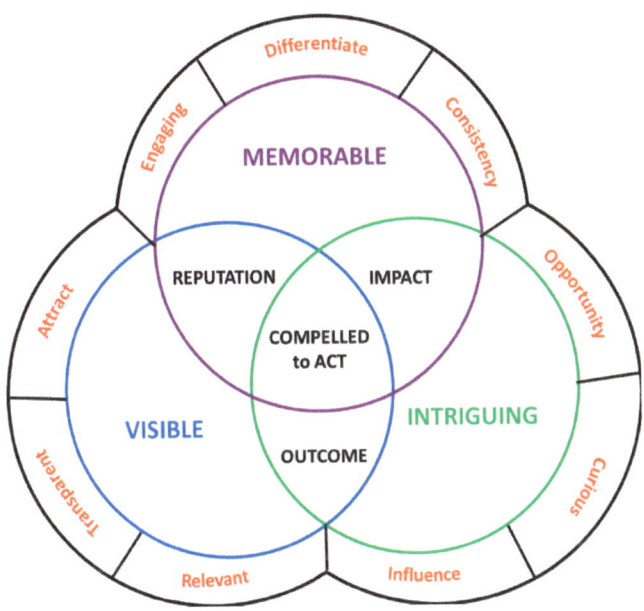

So, what can you do to make them feel like they are making the right decision and are compelled to act? How do you become compelling?

The first step is to determine what their pain points are.

Asking questions can reveal why they are still hesitant to make a decision. They may respond with, "I can't afford you," or "We're too busy to do this right now," or "I have had bad experiences in the past." It can sometimes be as blunt as, "Okay. If you're the expert, show me."

A useful tool to manage objections is the 'Feel, Felt and Found' technique. This can be based on your experiences or sharing a third party's story. The best-case scenario is when the third-party shares first-hand how they overcame similar objections.

The technique is essentially three-fold:

1. I understand how you feel (showing empathy).

2. I initially felt the way, as (insert your experience with their concern, so they know you understand, and you can help them resolve the situation).

3. However, I found that after doing X, then Y happened (X being the act you want them to be compelled to do, and Y being the positive outcome they will gain).

You can say or do many things; however, the most effective approach will be incorporating validations from others, particularly if they have engaged you in the past.

STEP 4: BE COMPELLING

Third party affirmation is a powerful way to give your prospects confidence to proceed.

Imagine if a third party said the following in front of an intrigued prospect?

"I understand how you feel. I initially felt the same, as I was concerned whether Gordon would be able to deliver what he promised. I had been burnt before and didn't want to waste money on yet another 'expert'. However, Gordon took me through a unique, yet logical 4-step process, and gave me the support I needed to learn the techniques. I now feel much more confident when networking, so much so that I have convinced my colleagues to undertake the same training."

Consider the last item you purchased online, or the latest movie you saw, or the last restaurant you dined at; the odds are that you learnt about it from a variety of sources, however your final decision was the result of an online review, a suggestion from a trusted source, or having had a previous positive experience. Like many people, if I have a choice between two movies, I will always visit a reliable movie review site to see which movie received the highest ratings. Why?

We want to make sure we're making the right decision based on the available information.

Even if an intrigued prospect doesn't actively seek out other people's opinions, they are still likely to want to base their decisions on as much factual data as they can find. Knowing this, you need to help them to easily find it. This is part of the final stage of Network with Purpose.

Won an award? Share a photo of you celebrating it with your team. Helped a client win an award? Get them to share it. Spoken in front of your peers? Video and post it on social media as proof of what you can do.

Motivated someone to become healthier? Get them to show their before-and-after photos. Have expertise in a subject? Write a book to help others.

STEP 4: BE COMPELLING

You can harness the power of the written word in several ways. Provide reassurance with a money-back guarantee, a KPI agreement to show that you stand behind your offer, or a written referral or testimonial. I like to refer individuals to recommendations I have received, such as:

"After only one session, Gordon helped me to see the importance of soft skills in building your profile, visibility and ultimately your practice, including using various types of networking to create and identify opportunities, and the importance of accountability to help you achieve your business goals. Thanks, Gordon - looking forward to putting this into action today!" - Phoebe Pitt, Mills Oakley Lawyers.

"Over time I was exposed to his strategic approach to business, his natural relationship-building skills, his commercial expertise, and the proven methodologies he uses to deliver business growth. It quickly became clear to me that he was a first-class operator. The tangible value Gordon delivered to the room was immense and widely acclaimed by all attendees, who left with a multitude of key takeaways to implement in their businesses. A consummate networker, Gordon constantly uses his connections and networks, always looking for ways to benefit others as both a business coach and mentor, and a connection. I cannot recommend him highly enough."
- Danny Innes, Newscorp.

Third party statements like these will cement your reputation as a person that people will want to network with, and more importantly, feel compelled to work with or join. They will feel compelled to board your plane and head to the ideal destination with you.

When I work directly with my clients, the compelling factor can also sometimes be the actual dilemmas I have committed to help them resolve. It may be the excitement around being able to expedite the consultative process by identifying a 'big' problem that can be solved within a short period of time, for a return that is many times more

STEP 4: BE COMPELLING

than the cost of the engagement. The allure of being able to solve a major pain point, in conjunction with you already being visible, memorable and intriguing, can be an intoxicating reason for a prospect to act.

This could be as simple as quickly helping them to generate more free time, something that most people would value. With my expertise, one client identified 30 extra hours a week to spend on business development, which in turn enabled the business to successfully pitch and undertake new opportunities, resulting in new business worth seven figures, over a 4-week period. In another instance I changed a list of 1,000 prospects into a list of 18,000 qualified clients in 6 weeks, simply by changing the way the opportunity was presented.

These are prime examples of having made an impact.

Will people choose the person or business that has little to show for their efforts, or the one that has made the most positive impact?

Do you want to work with an individual or business you have never heard of, or the one that everyone is talking about as the 'go to', the one people endorse as the reason for their success; the one that has transformed them from where they were, to where they want to be; and best of all, the one that was alongside them on their journey, as they learnt to Network with Purpose?

You now have the knowledge and guidance to Network with Purpose. You have the ability to go down the path that is right for you, and you can take others on the journey.

#Your Path. Our Journey.

But, having the path laid out before you is only part of the equation. Remember what got you to where you are right now, and what motivated you to want to learn more. The next step you take will define your future.

How deep is your desire to move forward and Network with Purpose?

IN MEMORIAM

In loving memory of Peter Jenkins

1940 – 2018

COPYRIGHT

First published in Australia by Gordon Jenkins, 2018

Copyright © Gordon Jenkins, 2018

Foreword by Marcel Kreis published by arrangement

The moral right of the author has been asserted

ISBN: 978-0-6483807-2-6

Gordon Jenkins, is the humorous and straight-talking international authority on visibility and business growth that helps entrepreneurs and professionals breakthrough their plateau. He helps these invisible go-getters become visible by networking with purpose and improving their business strategies, so they achieve sustainable business growth and personal life goals. Gordon is the supporter of the underdog; his purpose is to help ordinary people achieve extraordinary and meaningful outcomes, everyday.

Find out more about Gordon Jenkins and how to Network with Purpose – iamgordonjenkins.com

A contribution from the sale of each book supports The Lungitude Foundation - lungitude.com.au

www.ingramcontent.com/pod-product-compliance
Lightning Source LLC
Chambersburg PA
CBHW042051290426
44110CB00001B/30